Forgiveness and
Reparation,
the Healing Journey

theology
MY

Mpho Tutu van Furth

Forgiveness and Reparation, the Healing Journey

Fortress Press

Minneapolis

FORGIVNESS AND REPARATION,
THE HEALING JOURNEY

Originally published by Darton, Longman, and Todd
London, UK
Copyright © 2022 Mpho Tutu. Published by
Fortress Press, an imprint of 1517 Media. All rights
reserved.

Print ISBN: 978-1-5064-8455-6
eBook ISBN: 978-1-5064-8456-3

Cover design: Kristin Miller

Restitution: the return of something lost or stolen to its proper owner. Giving back what was taken.

Retribution: punishment inflicted on someone as vengeance for a wrong or criminal act.

Reparation: the action of making amends for a wrong one has done. Healing the breach.

Repair begins with a posture.
Imagine a liturgical dancer.
What shape would his body form to connote
*   humility?*
Head bowed. Shoulders slumped. Hands
*   achingly empty*
What is the gesture that admits
'I did this thing
that hurt your heart'?
Where does a body bend, or twist, to say, 'I am
*   sorry'?*
and what folds or stretches to plead, 'forgive me'?
imagine a dance where the movements cascade
*   hard and fast*
unable to contain their own urgency ...
or stutter tentative and slow
so unsure.
Would there be music ...
the slow low moan of anguish?

Or maybe just the percussion of feet on floor
and the hush and hiss of breath?
Imagine a liturgical dancer
with a needle and a golden thread
reaching out to repair
the ragged edges of peoples and generations
and years of hurt.

WE KNOW IT instinctively. We feel in our bones that what was taken can never be restored. And there is no payment that is an adequate price for even a single human life. On each side of our great divide we misconstrue the goal.

The white people pull out their spreadsheets trying to tally a total of misery minus the years between. What, they wonder, is the discount for that half step towards equality, that gesture at recompense? Affirmative action, set asides, preferential admissions that are handed out wrapped in resentment.

In a documentary the white girl sits next to the pool, the black servants gliding silently in and out of the frame to minister to her needs. 'I wasn't even alive in apartheid', she says. 'I didn't do anything. It wasn't my fault. Why must

9

I pay?' The irony of her circumstance slides past her eyes.

The older generation of white people is suspicious: 'This "reparation" is like a bribe. We pay now and for a moment you are silent. But you will be back. You or your children will come claiming it wasn't enough. We know you are right. How could it ever be enough? And because we know we can never pay enough we refuse to begin to pay.'

People of colour of every shade pull out catalogues of woe. Scrap books filled with unnamed ancestors and unborn children. They tell the family stories that never got written. They speak of demolished homes, demolished communities and displaced people. They speak of stolen youth, and stolen work. They speak of stolen land, and stolen hope. They speak of stolen lives. They speak of stolen voices. They speak of being silent or being silenced. They speak into the wind. And they create their own charts of resentment that no payment will erase.

'What about us?' the young man asked.

It was early days yet. South Africa's Truth and Reconciliation Commission was still unchallenged as a miracle of human healing both around the world and inside South Africa. 'What about me and people like me?

'My mother was an anti-apartheid activist, a freedom fighter. She was jailed, tortured, eventually killed. I was young. I didn't understand. I didn't know where my mother had gone. My grandmother raised me. When the Commission was set up she went there. She told her story about the daughter she lost. She faced the perpetrator. She forgave him. But what about me?

'I never told my story. Nobody ever heard me say how much I missed my mom. No one asked for my forgiveness. My grandmother told her story and granted her forgiveness. The perpetrator got amnesty and he was gone. I never even met him. I got nothing.'

LET'S BEGIN WITH the word, reparations. We read reparations. But we don't hear repair. One side hears the loud angry demand to return what was stolen. They hear the rancorous noise of protest before they see the faces in the crowd. They read reparations but it sounds like retribution and recompense, an ounce of gold for every ounce of flesh that was bought or sold; a salary, with compound interest for every unpaid or underpaid minute; an acre with interest for every acre taken. We read reparations but for each of us, wherever we stand the meaning of the word shifts like sand. We stand for one moment solidly certain of what reparations mean and what they must achieve and the next moment the ground slips away from under us as the wind of a new opinion blows. What seemed clear and simple is suddenly cloudy and complicated.

Complicated by all the people involved. Complicated by the lack of clarity about what reparations are designed to accomplish. Complicated by which of the raft of wrongs reparations are supposed to address. Because we disagree about the goal we disagree about the way to achieve the desired outcome. We wrestle with the idea of reparations sometimes in good faith, sometimes in bad faith. But we wrestle. And we bring all of our hopes, fears, worries and resentments to our wrestling. Our experience of the word now has everything to do with what we know and what we imagine of our ancestor's experience of life then.

So let us begin with the word. Let us turn our ears to hear it aright. Let us resolve to hearken to the music of it. Let us listen for multi-tonal melody of reparations. Let us listen for the jarring note of what is broken. And let us listen for the bright sound of what rings true. Maybe we can only hear reparations aright if embedded in the heart of reparations is love. The apostle Paul reminds us, 'If I speak in the tongue of mortals and of angels, but do not have

14

love, I am a noisy gong or a clanging cymbal ...'.
Reparations without love clang. The point and
purpose of reparations can only be healing and
love because what creation strains towards,
what all that is yearns towards, what salvation
bends towards is God and God is love. Love is
the point and the purpose of every life and is
all of the meaning of life. As the apostle Paul
says, 'If I give away all my possessions, and if
I hand over my body ... but do not have love, I
gain nothing.'

So reparations begin with a spiritual
posture: the posture of love. And reparations
must begin with a mental posture: the posture
of humility.

REPARATIONS ARE THEIR own healing liturgical dance. A dance in seven steps: the prelude in humility, setting aside the arrogance that has corseted us, stiffened our necks and held our heads aloft in pride we acknowledge the burden of wrong that bows our shoulders and bends our backs. The first step would speak the words 'I'm sorry' and in so saying open a door for the dance to begin. The next steps flow one into another, movement and stillness answering stillness and movement. Through the open door the dancer enters, leaning heavily on humility and remorse. Resting in their lap a perpetrator who is penitent could listen long to the stories of victims and their descendants and dare to hear the hurt that their actions and the actions of their ancestors have caused. When the story is told and the hurt is named, reparations are the thread offered that might make repair. Ask forgiveness, it will make the repair stronger: remorseful apology and reparation twined with gracious forgiveness, strands of hope woven together to make a better future than the one that the past promised us. Our future is learning together how better to love. We must learn how better to live love and how better to live in love. We must study how better to be love and how to embody love.

I hear the music of prelude. Come, let us dance.

If my people who are called by my name humble themselves, pray, seek my face, and turn from their wicked ways, then I will hear from heaven, and will forgive their sin and heal their land. (2 Chronicles 7:14)

Arrogance is a cage and a corset. Its bones and stays hold a body erect and unyielding. Rigid thinness in place of soft generosity.

There is something dignified about genuine humility. Maybe because genuine humility is born of an honest self-assessment and true self-acceptance. '*For by the grace given to me I say to everyone among you not to* **think** *of yourself more* **highly** *than you ought to* **think***, but to* **think** *with sober judgment, each according to the measure of faith that God has assigned.*' (Romans 12:3)

'We want to forgive them ... and perhaps they can forgive us.' She had to learn to walk again. Her body was no longer the lean lithe body that had walked into the golf club that fateful day. She was broken in places that do not heal. For months she could not feed, or bathe or clothe herself and her children had to help her with the most intimate tasks. She could have been bitter or bowed. Her voice could have dripped venom toxic enough to destroy the bodies of the young men who threw the hand grenades and fired the guns that brought her there. But instead of the twisted poverty of anger and despair she radiated the dignity of humility. And in time with dignity and humility she met the men whose attack ended her holiday party. With dignity and humility they met her.

19

Maybe it is the lack of humility that victims hear when the politicians say, 'I'm sorry'. The politicians sa, 'I'm sorry on behalf of cities and nations.' The response of the victims may be stony suspicion, open hostility, or cold indifference. The victims and their descendants say, 'We have heard this "sorry" so many times in so many ways and there is no remorse in it and it tastes of so much nothing that our appetite for the political sorry is dull. Over the years this "sorry" has broken so many promises that it has been emptied of hope. It rings hollow.' They turn away, their bodies etched with disdain.

'But we are sorry', different people stand up to repeat the refrain. Those hungry for a different relationship with the past and a different relationship between the descendants of the former masters and the descendants of subjected people snatch the words from the politicians' lips and examine them. They turn them over on their tongues. They bring to the words a teaspoonful of recognition ... there is a past that we have chosen not to know. There are stories we have stifled or chosen not to hear. After the recognition comes an ounce of knowledge then enough daring to stare down denial. We are sorry, we will unbury the history we have hidden. We will unearth the harms inflicted in our name. And we will face the truths that don't need to be unearthed for they are hidden in plain sight. Systemic evil, Richard Rohr calls these truths: the evil considered necessary to sustain the 'common good'. The systems of racism, sexism, ableism, homophobia and nativism that are woven into the fabric of society to secure life as we know it. The common good is clearly not good for everyone, it is only good for a vanishingly small some.

Humility speaks: 'We are sorry'. This 'we are sorry' will not stand on the dais dictating the terms of its own surrender. This 'we are sorry' will not try to define for the victims the edges of their experience. This 'we are sorry' will not lay upon those wronged the weight of expectation. You are not required to be gracious in response. We hope that you will hear that we are genuinely sorry.

The door is open. The dance begins.

*R*EMORSE SITS IN *humility for the most onerous duty*
We cannot heal you
We can only hear you
We can only let you speak and we can listen
We can only be still and see you dance your
    stories
the ones you shared before
the ones that we half heard or chose to ignore
the ones handed like tarnished treasures from the
mouths of grandparents into grandchildren's
    hands
the ones unspooling into this moment
Remorse will stay for the dance until the dance
    is done
until the winding thread of story is unspun
though every step and pirouette throws up
    shards of our shame
we will be silent
    and we will stay

THE STORIES CAN fill books and years.

'The day before they came to demolish our house in District Six we cleaned. Me and my mother on our hands and knees scrubbing the floor and polishing ... with that wax polish, you know, you spread it and let it dry dull and then you come back with a brush and a cloth and buff until it shines. And we washed the windows, vinegar and newspaper, the old way. That house was sparkling. We found my mother the next morning. She killed herself. Her body lay on that clean kitchen floor.'

'The policeman came on horseback to get my father. He tied him to the horse and forced him to run behind it. He was going to make him run all the way to town. I remember my mother throwing stones at the horse. The policeman

25

had to get down the horse was bucking and rearing so. It's funny now. My mother was so rash, so angry, so brave.'

'When the soldiers came everyone tried to get into our car. We must have been fifteen people in a vehicle meant to sit five. My nose was pressed against the windscreen so I couldn't look away. I had to watch as the soldiers, faceless behind their helmets, in riot gear with plastic shields and sjamboks whipped my sister and her boyfriend. I can't describe my rage.'

'They would come at three a.m. Surrounding the house they would shine their torches through all the windows at once and bang on the door "Police, open up." I don't even remember how many times it happened. It was just the three of us, me and my brother and my mother. I was eight or nine, my brother was much younger. They would turn the house upside down, emptying drawers and cupboards; searching under the bed. They would say they were looking for my father. They knew he was dead. They killed him. They killed him because he was an activist. We didn't know that yet. We didn't know that he was dead. They killed him and burnt his body.'

'I was sentenced to 14 years imprisonment on Robben Island in the 1960s. After my release, I was detained frequently and tortured on each occasion. There's what they called the helicopter method of torturing. They suffocated me by pulling a mask over my face. With the helicopter method they put a stick behind your knees and you were hung upside down. Whilst this was happening you were suffocated. Every time I was released they would come back and harass me. I couldn't work. My wife had to be the breadwinner. Then they burnt down my house. They arrested my son too. He died in jail. They poured acid on him and he died.'

The bare earth around the shipping container was swept and tidy. The teacher was wearing a crisp white shirt. An oasis of neat orderliness amid the haphazard construction of tin shacks. 'No, we don't get books. The government doesn't give us books. We borrow them from the school across the highway. The government doesn't consider this a school because this is a shanty town, an informal settlement, a place where people come and build the homes that the government won't build. The government calls them, "unnecessary appendages". The women and children are unnecessary appendages to their husbands and fathers. The men must be here to work for the white people but their families are unnecessary. They are supposed to go to the homelands. This is a school that the government says is not a school. We are teachers that the government doesn't pay. How do we get paid? We get paid from the children's school fees. Well, if they don't have money for fees that month we are volunteers.'

'It was raining when they came. My husband had gone working. It was raining. They came anyhow. All of our belongings piled up in the mud. And the home we built ... yes, it was a shack made from scrap metal collected from here and there. It was a shack but we lived there together so it was home. They flattened our home. My children and me loaded on a lorry like cattle. Taken and dumped in a place they called a homeland though it was far from home.'

It wasn't all huge, defining traumas. The little indignities have been their own cascade. The slip of a white boy addressing my father – all thirty plus years, two college degrees and an ordination certificate of him – that preteen addressing my father as 'boy'; or my dad, as Dean and senior pastor at the cathedral – the cardinal parish in Johannesburg – being directed by the doorman to the tradesman's entrance when he went to pay a pastoral visit to one of his congregants. Not a trauma drama, just the casual disdain of the white women who expected my mother to step off the sidewalk so they could pass. Not a trauma, just the deliberate indignity of going to the stores that served their black clientele only through a service window and would not let them inside – no black people stepped inside except to mop the floors and give the white people tea. Not a drama or a disgrace, just the disregard of the employers who insisted on anglicised names or renamed their servants because 'African names are too hard to pronounce' while the oppressed somehow managed to form their mouths around foreign tongues. It wasn't all huge, defining traumas. It was just the dailiness of having our dignity turned to dust.

Listen to the stories. And those were just some of the recent ones, the ones in living memory.

What of the ones before? When they took our land and sickened our cattle and enslaved our people? What of the women they carried away to foreign lands, to be poked, prodded examined and displayed naked as if they were not human beings but exotic beasts? What of the thousands driven from farming the land into the darkness down the mines? And before that what of the people the Europeans portrayed from their earliest encounters with Africans, the dignified dark people in European paintings; kings, queens and their retinues, warriors and their wives. Avarice and greed recoloured Africans in the European mind. The wealth of the continent and the desire for conquest distorted the white person's vision and erased every trace of nobility from the African form so they portrayed Africans as brutes and beasts.

And what of the woes that wander into this moment? What of the poor education, unless you are rich or you win a scholarship that affords you the privilege of rising before dawn to drive all the miles from the township to town to sit in a classroom next to the white children who rolled out of bed twenty minutes ago and can walk home to lunch ... and you still have the miles to go home to do your chores before staying up late, with uncertain electrical power, to do the homework that you must have ready when you rise before dawn to drive all the miles ...? And what of the inadequate health care with the doctor who sets an appointment time of eight a.m. with no consideration for the fact that public transport is unreliable so you will wake up before the sun to walk to the taxi rank and sit in the minibus taxi praying that enough passengers will arrive before the hour is eaten so that the driver will get on the road and you will be in time for the train that will take you to the bus that will take you to the taxi that will get you to the hospital at eight a.m. in time for the doctor who will make you wait until ten a.m. because the sun was shining and it seemed like a good day for a golf round or a car wash? Or discriminatory hiring and predatory lending that plague us into the present day? What of the consequences in limited opportunity, straitened circumstance, poverty, criminality, violence, diminished life and excess death? What of the thankless hard labour of constantly challenging stereotypes, not living but striving to throw off the defining label that misnames you where every misstep sends you sliding down the scale of unfair expectations; how taxing to choose when the only open options are perfection or failure and good enough is not good enough? What of the stress of struggling to be seen not as a statistic but as a human being? Where do we place these in our stories?

Sit a while with your sorry. Our pain has something to say.

I DON'T WANT to hear how I have hurt you
Your words sear like firebrands
they pummel like stones
shame rises up to suffocate me
I want you to stop
so
I
can
breathe
But I must hear how I have hurt you
I owe you open eyes to see your pain
I owe you open ears to hear your pain
I owe you heart open to feel your pain
I owe you stillness
and silence
Though your stories pierce me like a thousand
    needles
I will not throw up a storm of words in my own
    defence

I will watch
I will listen
I will hear
I will allow your pain to find a home in me
It will teach me how to honour your humanity
How to cherish your dignity

I NEVER SAW his face, never knew who he was. I could only hear from his voice that he was young, maybe ten or twelve. I was imprisoned in the cell next to his. I heard his screams and pleas as they tortured him. First I blocked my ears to try to shut out the sound. It was terrifying and agonising at once. But then I thought I must bear witness. There is nothing I can do for him except to bear witness and to pray. In time the screams fell silent.

*L*ISTEN AND HEAR. *I cannot parse out my pain in the crisp staccato of a tap dance, feet too well shod to feel the stage.*

I do this dance on broken glass.

I do this dance where it is dark.

I do this dance to seek out my pain. I know the words but not the steps that spell shame.

And sadness. And anguish. And grief.

I don't know how to dance self-doubt or pose the question out loud 'Am I not a child of God? Tell me, am I not?'

I do this dance on broken glass.

I do this dance in here the dark.

I do this dance to hide my pain and the steps to the letters that spell out shame and heartsickness and heart-soreness and bone-weariness, fatigue.

I do this dance on broken glass.

I do this dance where it is dark.

I do this dance to seek out my pain. I am
searching for the letters that spell my name.
I want to reclaim who I was meant to be, not
a defective you but a perfect me. My dark
skin God's kiss not God's rebuke. I dance to
pound away your distortions of the truth.
I know the dance of terror and fear.
I know that one well, I learned it here at your
hands under the whip you wielded or was
it the noose or the bullet or the bomb or the
burning.
I do this dance on broken glass.
I do this dance here in the dark.
I dance in darkness so you must strain, you
must be determined to see my pain. You
must want enough for things to change that
you will sit witness not once but once and
again, and again, and again.

I T IS HUMILITY, not humiliation, that can sit and wait while eyes adjust to the darkness. It is contrition, not comeuppance or disgrace, that can sit and wait and listen to the stories and heed the hurt. It is repentance and remorse that can bear the sounds and the silence. It is repentance and remorse that can bear to be the silence. It is repentance and remorse that can bear to hold the sounds. It is humility and hope that bring us here. It is humility and hope that let us dare to believe that there can be a repair.

It's reparations, not forgiveness, that pave the way to repair.

WE ENDED OUR dance sweaty, spent,
yearning for a grain of hope
And you stood before us with your bottomless
   bowls
begging for a new beginning
So we danced again, weaving forgiveness out of
   air
because we knew that the future was locked in
   there
and we believed you would take that seed
and grow from it a new way of being
but you took our forgiveness as a key
that unlocked your chains and set you free
we will not do that dance again
the stage is yours
you must begin

YOUR TEARS AND our tears have washed the floor clean. We danced and you watched and you listened to our stories and our pain. And we saw it was searing. Don't ask for forgiveness now ... handing us your request like Magi bearing gifts for the birth of a just relationship. 'Forgive me' is no gift. It is the empty box which you expect the powerless to fill with their forgiveness, the new tribute paid to the old rules. 'Forgive me' is no gift. 'Forgive me' is the dancer in the banquet hall prancing her steps lightly along tables laden with bounty. The tables groan under the weight they must bear. Life, work, name, pride, home, hope, dignity, culture, history, craft and creativity tossed casually under heaps of land and liberty, jostling piles of spices and mineral wealth, agricultural wealth, wild animal wealth and environmental health tossed on piles

45

of national identity. You have taken once or a thousand times and now you come to take again grabbing at forgiveness, one more decorative dipping bowl for your banquet table.

But we have done that dance. We have rushed onto the stage, our hearts heavy with hurt, our feet light with hope. We have stepped into the spotlight carrying fragrant forgiveness in generous hands and claimed the adulation of the audience that we so richly deserved. And while we danced our forgiveness you slipped into soft darkness drawing your banquet table behind you. And we remained on stage, soloists dancing a pas de deux.

Rend your hearts, not your garments. (Joel 2:13)

Our tears and yours have washed the floor clean. You danced and we watched and we listened to your stories and your pain. And it was searing. We do not ask for forgiveness now. We have asked and we have taken. We have taken, grabbed and grasped. We have grasped and we have stolen ... life, work, name, pride, home, hope, dignity, culture, history, craft and creativity, land and liberty, spices and mineral wealth, agricultural wealth, wild animal wealth and environmental health and national identity. And you have given your stories and your pain. We would not stand before you wanting more again. Humbly we come before you bearing our offering. Our hands are full of a new sorry now. This is no stiff-necked sorry seeking safety from a reckoning. This is the humble sorry of a contrite heart.

I DO THIS dance on holy ground
I do this dance to the sound of your stories
ringing in my ears
to the sound of my determined deafness through
all the years
to the sound of your anguish
to the sound of your tears
I do this dance on a thousand floors your
grandmothers scrubbed on bleeding knees
through a thousand doors of opportunity
that were slammed in faces of your fathers
and your brothers and your sisters and your
mothers
in the light that penetrated the windows of a
thousand prison cells
for a thousand years of protest
I do this dance on holy ground
I do this dance to the sound of your stories
ringing in my ears

*to the sound of my determined deafness through
all the years
to the sound of your anguish
to the sound of your tears
I do this dance on a thousand fresh cut lawns
that your grandfathers clipped with wizened
hands
across a thousand acres of ancestral land
that were robbed from your mothers and given
to mine
At the hallowed doors to a thousand rooms
where the fates of you and yours
were decided by me and mine
I do this dance on holy ground
I do this dance to the sound of your stories
ringing in my ears
to the sound of my determined deafness through
all the years
to the sound of your anguish
to the sound of your tears
that have softened my heart after
a thousand years
and worn a thousand holes in my pride
and uncovered the compassion that was hidden*

inside

the granite rock of fear from which my superiority

was carved

W E COME TO this hallowed ground knowing that if we want the well to be repaired we must bring bricks for the building.

'I survived days and nights of horrendous torture. I wept. I screamed. I whimpered. I prayed. I was not brave. I was not strong. I was terrified. There were times when I felt that the pain would never end. But there was a moment when they were torturing me that I experienced a shining clarity. I thought about my torturers and I knew we must help them to recover their humanity.'

We must recover our humanity. Not just the torturers, but the everyday 'just living by the (unjust) rules (that benefit me)' people. We must recover our humanity. We will begin by unearthing 'I am sorry' from the hidden corner where we stashed it under an edifice of accomplishment achieved at another's expense. We will take it from the mouths of prideful politicians and sample it ourselves. We have feared that 'I am sorry' would taste bitter on the tongue, the acrid acknowledgment that we were wrong, but once honestly uttered, flavour is something more like courage and healing seasoned with reality.

We must recover our humanity. We cannot hide endlessly from the past. We cannot hear your stories and believe that in listening and truth telling we have done enough to deserve a slate wiped clean of guilt. We cannot believe that for looking and listening we are owed a new reality shorn of responsibility for the debts of the past that are still eating our future.

We must recover our humanity. We must look in the mirror your stories hold and see how greed and lies have deformed us. Grabbing for glory we have become hungry ghosts ready to reach into every corner of the world to define as God's favour our filching and falsehoods, and finding ourselves monstrous in our own madness we have veiled every mirror that shows truth. 'I'm not a racist'; 'It was an empty land'; 'My people built this with their bare hands'; 'I didn't benefit'; 'I earned everything I own'; 'We paid for this with beads and brandy ... and a begging bowl'; 'I didn't know'; 'I never heard': In the face of every accusation we have thrown a storm of words that have sounded like a real defence but have only served to bend us further away from our humanity further from truth, beauty and reality.

We must recover our humanity. We can begin with the words, 'I am sorry'. The words start to untwist something that was gnarled and warped. It starts to pull apart the carapace that hardened on our hearts.

We must recover our humanity. Not each of us individually. But all of us together. Together we must challenge the insidiousness of evil and sin that convinces us again and again that each of us can and each of us must find our individual path to the sweetness of salvation. Evil and sin beguile us again and again with their ever-changing form, like a snake formed from smoke they slide away from us at every moment. The system of sin is too vast, too intertwined, too matted and enmeshed for any one of us to tackle it alone. We hack at one head but the hydra is born. Any and every one of us can be committed to rooting out the evil from our little lives but the systems that undergird our ways of being pin us down like knives that conspire to thwart us at every turn.

'White clergyman that I am I did not want to participate in the systemic evil of apartheid. I decided that I would not go where my black, coloured and Indian colleagues were not welcome. It seemed simple enough. I would only go to the more expensive "International" restaurants ... very infrequently on my salary. I would not join a gym but would exercise outside. I would not go to the segregated beaches. But it got harder quickly; where would I go for a haircut? Or a hospital stay? And what of housing? I, alone, could not untangle the web of apartheid. We had to do it together.'

We must recover our humanity. Each and all of us. Starting with the sorry that is more than just a word. Apology is a disposition of soul that remakes the world. 'I am sorry' shuts the mouth of defensive lies and admits the truth that fear and pride denies. And 'I am sorry' is the first share of bricks needed to make repair.

We must recover our humanity. 'I am sorry' begins the recovery. And then for the next step in the dance to begin we must bring an offering. So many times we have come bearing answers. Offering as gifts what we were ready to give up. Like Jacob, sending ahead of us what wealth we were willing to concede so we could retain the power we were not willing to yield. But this time is different because you have danced in darkness and we have strained, we have been determined to see your pain. We have wanted enough for things to change that we have sat witness not once but once and again, and again, and again. And now instead of telling you what debt we will pay we have finally come to ask you to say what is the medicine you need to begin the healing.

We come here to this holy ground feet unshod hearts truly bound and determined to atone for the harms that we have done. We cannot tell you what you will need from us to heal the wounds of years. We can only ask and then we can begin.

As we begin to recover our humanity we begin to see and know that the injuries we dealt to you hurt us too. We have come to know that the whip that bit your back stripped a sliver of softness from our hearts. We must say at last that every ounce of weariness that you bore at our expense also wore away our access to true joy. We must see and we must know that every time we imagined you as 'less than' something else inside of us was broken. We must see and we must know that the bricks we bring to make a repair are not just our share in healing you but are also building us anew. Through generations, decades, months and years we have sold our souls to buy our lives. But the angry ghosts of generations past and the seeds of generations yet unborn, your children and ours, have risen up to speak to us to reclaim their lives and to weigh our souls if what was broken is not repaired they will find our souls wanting.

We come offering reparations because we have finally come to know that reparations may never repay, but they will repair. Reparations will repair not only what is broken between us, but also what is broken in us. We have finally come to know and see that when we stole from you your humanity we did not become superhuman as we believed. But instead what we stole from you turned around and robbed us too. It is not a promise but it is a hope that the reparation we make to you may yet repair us too.

We must recover our humanity. We must dance the dance that sets us free from the hungry ghosts and the angry ghosts and the threat of generations yet unborn who scream at us, from before and beyond, of their right to form a future. We must dance that dance that draws us into the light that strips us bare of every air of misplaced pride and snobbery and lands us, finally, in the place of love. We must dance the dance that makes it safe to have mirrors on every side, the dance that lets us stand with our eyes open wide to acknowledge who we have been, who we are and who we can be. We must dance this dance that lets us hope for healing that allows to touch the feeling of being open to the possibility that value of life is not measured in things and that human worth is not a tally of units of clothing food and work. We dance the dance that lets us see that the value of human life is humanity.

We dance this reparation dance. We dance this dance that looks like loss, of things that we can calculate and count: we dance bringing caps and cash, coaches and coins, we carry dresses and diamonds and deserted homes. We dance to hand back what we claimed as our own. We dance to hand over what does not now and never really did belong to us, and though we relished the having it was never ours to have. We dance finally knowing and knowing well that whatever we must hand over and whatever we must hand back are worth every penny and carat and every yard, every year and every house and haunt. We dance this dance of reparation to create a more just dispensation for all.

We have danced the dance of greedy desperation. We have been the dancers in the banquet hall prancing our steps lightly along tables laden with bounty. The tables groaning under the weight they must bear. Your lives and work, your names and pride, your homes, your hope, your dignity, your culture, your history, your craft and creativity tossed casually under heaps of your land and liberty, jostling piles of spices and mineral wealth, agricultural wealth, wild animal wealth and environmental health tossed on piles of your national identity. We have taken once or a thousand times but now come to you hands open wide to yield what has decked our lives without adorning, what has filled our houses but left us empty, what has promised us safety from want and delivered the anxiety of always wanting for safety.

We dance to release every stolen thing that fills our lives without satisfying our hunger. We dance to restore the wholeness in you and that can begin to restore us to wholeness. We dance to repair every broken relationship that is a token of our own brokenness. We dance for we know we cannot have a whole relationship with un-whole people. When you become whole and wholly able to participate in a flourishing world you open the space for us to become whole and wholly able to participate in creating a world of flourishing as well.

We dance to release what is tainted with grief and pain to make of what is beautiful a celebration of skill and talent again. We dance to open the door for justice to reign between us, around us and within us again. We dance to slay the demons that the past created, the demons that have adopted us and given us their own names. We dance to be sure that those devils are slain that have inhabited the space that joy can claim when a world is created where justice reigns.

The old ones laid forgiveness at our feet, like an accolade for the prima ballerina. They paid us the tribute because we danced our truth, we told our stories of stealing their worth. They filled our stage with the flowers of hope, trusting us to respond to their gift in like manner, with grace. They didn't expect us to walk away. The old ones laid forgiveness at our feet like seeds of a forest that would blossom in peace. We took the gift but we did not plant the trees. The old ones laid forgiveness at our feet like medicine for our deepest need. We took the magic potion and tainted it with greed, grabbing this gift we denied all of us the chance to heal.

We do this dance of reparation this dance of gratitude and desperation. We dance to acknowledge what we have been given. We dance a fresh opportunity to restore to us both our humanity. We dance in all humility. We dance to ask what you will need to repair the breach that we have opened and cannot close alone. We dance to ask how and then we dance to begin to atone for harms we and ours inflicted and the wrongs we have done that have damaged you and yours and the world we share. We dance the dance of reparation and repair.

W HAT DO WE know of repair?
We know it from the lives we live daily
in the homes we inhabit with people we love
dearly
in the spaces where friendship creates the safety
to explore our own brokenness and despair.
What do we know of repair?
we know it from the people who see us when it
is safe to own the worst of ourselves
they are the ones who deserve the best of
ourselves
because they give us the freedom to be all of
ourselves
and inch ever closer to blessed dream of
ourselves
the beauty God sees when God sees us.
What do we know of repair?
We know from our friendships and our loves
that the reparations demanded when anger is

speaking

may shift when anger is satisfied by
    acknowledgement

and trust sees us return not just once but
    once and again to the work of remaking our
    relationships

What do we know of repair?

We know that it is not shaped by the perpetrator's
    leading

We know that only the victim can describe
    perfectly

the shape and form of the injury

and what it will take to heal.

What do we know of repair?

We know that when we begin God will meet us
    there.

Behold I make all things new. (Revelation 21:5)

Please forgive me.

When the payment of reparations has begun

these words have such a different tone

than the demand made when 'Forgive me' was
    paired with 'I'm sorry' and formed the whole

of the healing dance.
When the words 'I am sorry' begin the dance
    and reparations take their own place on the
    stage then
'Forgive me' can be a hope founded in mutuality.

‘I'M SORRY. FORGIVE ME.' They came, the men who had once wielded the power of life and death and every anguish in between. They came to tell their stories and their truth. They came with a profession and a plea. 'I am sorry. Forgive me.' They came, the men in their neat tight suits confessing their cruelty begging for a second chance. 'I have been tormented by what I have done. I am sorry. Forgive me.' They spoke these words into the faces of the women who had once been powerless. They said these words to the widows who howled their grief unable to contain the searing pain of their losses. They said these words to the children who had forgotten the scent of their mother and could only vaguely remember her smile and had lost the tunes to the lullabies she sang. They said these words to the ones who begged for even a bone of their father to bury and those once powerful men would tell that the fathers' bodies had been eaten through with acid or burned to hide the crime. 'I am sorry. Forgive me' they said to the men who had lost eyes to torture and to men who had almost lost their minds. They said the words to the boys with broken limbs and to the boy who had fled into exile only to languish in remote refugee camps and watch hope evaporate with the lengthening days. They said 'Forgive me' to the girls they stripped bare and forced to sit naked in windowless cells the ones who didn't dare to explain what had happened to them because they carried the shame even though they were the heroes and these men were to blame. They pleaded 'Forgive me' to the mothers who watched on the nightly news the heartbreaking images of their entrapped sons' lifeless bodies dragged in the dust like the carcasses of dead dogs. To all these who carried pain and pain to spare they spoke these words as if they would repair what had been damaged or destroyed. 'I am sorry. Forgive me.' And for a moment suspended in time it seemed that the tables were turned and the roles reversed. It seemed that power had found a new home in the laps of poor aunties who wore blankets around their waists, whose shoes did not click – chic heels on the tiled floor – but sloughed, cheap slippers and thick socks to keep warm. A procession of once powerful men faced the formerly powerless women. They came to beg. 'I am sorry. Please forgive me.'

'I'm sorry. Forgive me' the policemen said and soldiers the rapists and torturers said. It was a mountain in a mouthful for those saying the words. They extracted the pleas from their own mouths as painfully, it seemed, as they had once extracted confessions from the people they tortured. 'I am sorry. Forgive me.' To those sitting on the other side the words seemed so much easier to swallow than the pride the powerful had to choke down in order make a request of those they counted as powerless. So very few words that barely described the nightmare lives on the other side. 'I am sorry. Forgive me' and they imagined that would be payment in full for the weeks of torture of some had to endure, or the months of the torment of wondering if their loved one was alive, or years desperately searching for someone who had already died.

'I am sorry. Forgive me' were the words the perpetrators said. I am taking responsibility for what I did and what was done at my command or in my name. But what the victims heard was not the same. They didn't hear the words the perpetrators said. They heard the words of the translators instead. 'Ndicela uxolo.' But that's not the same.

The English 'I am sorry' wraps the plea in the logic of individuality and the English 'Forgive me' underlines the same. What I have done was done only by me and thus is only my responsibility. This 'I am sorry. Forgive me' is all about me.

But the old ones heard a different word. 'Ndicela uxolo' means 'I ask for peace'. It is an ubuntu apology and it is about we. 'I ask for peace' sees our interconnectivity.

'I am sorry. Forgive me' means set me free

of the guilt and the shame that has burdened me. Decide to wipe the debt slate clean for me.

The old ones heard 'I ask for peace' and they offered forgiveness as peace based on ubuntu reciprocity. They gave their forgiveness as space to plants the seeds of a better future for the whole community.

Ubuntu: the African philosophy of reciprocity. A person is a person through other persons. I am because you are.

When the old ones heard Ndicela uxolo. I ask for peace. Ubuntu peace is peace between us and peace within each of us. Ubuntu forgiveness is peace that heals. The once powerful men told of their own torment. They told of guilt and shame and sleepless nights. They spoke of the haunting of those they had killed and the haunting of those who yet lived. They spoke of the sickness that stalked them. They spoke of depression, anxiety and the disbelief that they could be so inhumane. They spoke of their suffering family relationships and of not trusting themselves to be the husbands and fathers they wanted to be. They spoke of their own silences and rages and fact that peace had fled from them. They asked forgiveness and the old ones heard them ask for peace. When the old ones heard Ndicela uxolo they did not hear a request directed at an individual me. They heard perpetrators asking for hope for a better 'we'. They heard an appeal for healing for all of us and the space between us that is community. They heard an appeal for a healing of the fabric of life. A healing for themselves and their children. A healing for perpetrators and their progeny.

Without reparations 'I am sorry. Forgive me' asks victims to pick up an eraser and walk through the past eradicating the injuries that perpetrators inflicted so that those who wielded the scythe of destruction can be released from the guilt for their cruelty and their greed, their prejudice and violence, while preserving the benefits that their behaviour has bestowed on them and their children. Without reparations forgiveness has no ubuntu, and it heals nothing. It does not heal the victim and it holds no medicine for the perpetrator.

The old ones offered not forgiveness but uxolo, peace. And the peace the old ones offered healed the past and built a new future.

'Peace, is not the absence of conflict, peace is the presence of justice.'

The Revd Dr Martin Luther King Jr.

The ubuntu understanding of forgiveness is that forgiveness cultivates justice and bestows peace.

The forgiveness we offered you was the one to make all things new to tear away the tangled weeds and make the garden that brought us peace. The forgiveness we once offered you would build justice where cruelty had lived. Our forgiveness was born and bred in ubuntu. Later we came to understand and see that forgiveness for you had its home in individuality and could not understand the logic of community. So forgiveness for you was what set you free of all responsibility for us.

But reparations have made a new place for us to gather. Reparations have started to reveal what it takes for all of us to heal and to step into God's new creation.

I AM SORRY
Please forgive me
It sounds so different now
it is no longer a demand to which I must bow so
that you can retain your power
I am sorry. Forgive me
It is not the same request you made
when I had told my story, wept and prayed that
you would listen and feel
more than my words could ever tell of torment
and sadness and all my woe
and you wanted me to grant your forgiveness so
that you could go on and forget that the past was
a story we shared and that something was owed
to make a new world.
I am sorry. Please forgive me
when first you have told your truth and walked
towards me and asked what I need for a new
beginning

77

that is a dose healing before any other deed is done
Then I am sorry. Please forgive me
sounds like genuine plea to walk together into a changed relationship and a new way of being that can make of us and our world a new community.

We must learn to love. Love not as a feeling that comes and goes according to its own whim but love as a way of life that takes account of all of life. Reparations begin to put us in touch with that kind of love. Every other way of being privileges me and mine and insists on grabbing the best and the most. It is the way we have operated not only to the detriment of people but also to the destruction of our planet. We have claimed a logic of love but have lived a logic of lordship and greed. Lordship over each other and lordship over all creation. We have claimed a God who died for our salvation but lived like gods who have no regard for the health, flourishing and wellbeing of any beyond our smallest circle of concern. We don't quite know how to live in love. The longer we live in the kind of world we have created the farther we slip from the possibility of learning to live

MY THEOLOGY — MPHO TUTU VAN FURTH

in love, more and more of us subscribe to the logic of lordship craving for ourselves the riches that have wrested from the hands of the many to rest in hands of the vanishingly few. We are ailing. And the sickness is contagious. We spread the contagion through all of our media teaching each to dream of joining the few who have what they don't need at the expense of the many who don't have what they truly need.

We must learn to love. God keeps holding out this invitation to us to live a more perfect world, a world of love. It is not an impossible vision. It is a vision of flourishing that can and could be within reach for each and all of us. We are invited to live an ethic of family. We are challenged by the ethic of family because it gainsays the ethic of deserving that we imagine that we live by. In truth we do not get what we deserve. We can only pray that continues to be the case. What has anyone we ever done to deserve life breath or sunshine?

We must learn to love. We must learn to love those least like us. We must learn to want for those we fear the best that we wish for ourselves. We must learn that in this world there is enough and more than enough for each and all of us to live in peace. To seek peace and pursue it we must chase away our greed.

We must learn to love. We crave the joy that love can bring but we are unwilling to do the thing that brings love and joy. We struggle to take account of the hungry other. The person who God has given us as sister, brother, sibling in this world. We draw our circle of concern so unconscionably small that barely anyone fits in there at all. They must look like us and pray like us. They must love like us or learn like us. They must dress like us and be like us in order for them to matter to us. This is not what God asks of us:

Is not this the kind of fasting I have chosen:
to loose the chains of injustice
and untie the cords of the yoke,
to set the oppressed free
and break every yoke?

Is it not to share your food with the hungry

and to provide the poor wanderer with shelter –
when you see the naked, to clothe them,
and not to turn away from your own flesh and
blood?

Then your light will break forth like the dawn,
and your healing will quickly appear;
then your righteousness will go before you,
and the glory of the Lord will be your rear guard.

Then you will call, and the Lord will answer;
you will cry for help, and he will say: Here am I.
If you do away with the yoke of oppression,
with the pointing finger and malicious talk,

and if you spend yourselves in behalf of the
*   hungry*
and satisfy the needs of the oppressed,
then your light will rise in the darkness,
and your night will become like the noonday.

The Lord will guide you always;
he will satisfy your needs in a sun-scorched l
*   and*

and will strengthen your frame.
You will be like a well-watered garden,
like a spring whose waters never fail.

Your people will rebuild the ancient ruins
and will raise up the age-old foundations;
you will be called Repairer of Broken Walls,
Restorer of Streets with Dwellings.

(Isaiah 58)

This is why reparations. Not as payment. Not as punishment. But as help, hope and healing. A step in the direction of a world of love.

We have considered reparations as their own healing liturgical dance. Humility drifted in bringing healing and the courage to admit that a wrong has laid waste to the space between us. 'I am sorry' with no breath of expectation cleared the stage and opened the space for the dance to begin. Remorse could take a solo turn, dancing the support for stories to be told and told again. Remorse could stand the pain of listening to pain and holding a vigil for the wounding that pride and

83

cruelty caused. Humility and courage, remorse and heeding craft a thread that one can offer to make repair. The offer of reparations is an offer of healing for all who have been touched by the injuries of the past that cast their long shadows into the present and threaten the future. Only when reparations are being made can forgiveness be asked with any measure of good faith. Reparations are not the price paid for forgiveness, forgiveness is grace. The forgiveness Christ models for us drives us deeper into relationship. It is not the forgiveness that frees us to walk away. It is the forgiveness that truly frees us to stay and together craft a future. Our future is learning together how better to love. We must learn how better to live love and how better to live in love. We must study how better to be love and how to embody love.

*R*epair begins with a hope and a promise and
Repair begins with a posture.
Remember the liturgical dancer.
see the shape his body formed to connote
    humility?
Head bowed. Shoulders slumped. Hands
    achingly empty
see that sad sweet gesture that admits
'I did this thing
that hurt your heart'?
Watch how that body bends, or twists, to say, 'I
    am sorry'?
and notice what folds or stretches to plead,
'forgive me'?
remember this dance where the movements
    cascaded hard and fast
unable to contain their own urgency ...
and how they sometimes stuttered tentative and
    slow

85

so unsure.
There was music ...
the slow low moan of anguish?
And the hellish howl of grief
And there was the percussion of feet on floor
and the hush and hiss of breath?
remember that liturgical dancer
with a needle and a golden thread
reaching out to repair
the ragged edges of peoples and generations
and years of hurt.